A PATH TO SELF

© 2013, Martine Garcin-Fradet
Edition : BoD - Books on Demand
12/14 rond-point des Champs Elysées
75008 Paris
Imprimé par Books on Demand GmbH,
Norderstedt, Allemagne
ISBN : 9782322033287
Dépôt légal : Août 2013

Transpersonal Psychology

Martine Garcin-Fradet

A PATH TO SELF

Accompanied Inner Communication,

Translated by Ann King

A PATH TO SELF

A PATH TO SELF

This book is the synthesis of my work detailed in my previous books. My objective is to explain the elaboration of an unknown yet very promising accompaniment technique. I am talking about CPA, in English "Accompanied Inner Communication". By accompanying the hand over a computer keyboard, expression emerges from a part of ourselves that we do not usually have access to.

Etymologically, communicate comes from the Latin *communicare*, which means "to share something, to pool together". Communication is an inherent phenomenon that human beings enjoy when they meet. In essence, Man is a communicating being and from the beginning of humanity, pooling together life experiences was obtained through drawings, cave engravings; and gestures.

From birth, the human being is immersed in a communicating bath; he cannot develop without these stimulations. Communication with the newborn baby largely takes place via touching and physical contact. The recent experience regarding Romanian orphanages proved that the total lack of physical contact brought on serious growth delays, even a large number of deaths of newborn babies.

Accompanied Inner Communication associates words with touching, by establishing contact and cupping the accompanied person's hand. This communication is above all a welcome, allowing each accompanied person to better structure himself and live his own life. Listening in Accompanied Inner Communication is connecting the person to himself, to his inner self.

The words that emerge from this accompaniment are the reflection of a **feeling** and in no way at all can be considered information. Experiments have shown that when five people are present at an accident and they are asked to testify, none of the testimonies are the same. Similarly the way an event registers within us and activates an emotional experience is subjective and colored by the feelings that are specific to each of us. Such an emotional experience can emerge in Accompanied Inner Communication. It has no value as information – it is not a fact.

The objective of our accompanying work is to facilitate the emergence of an aspect of the past as it was recorded by the person who is consulting so that he/she can live the present with increased consciousness. It is not about rummaging around in the past but rather letting emerge what the person needs at that specific moment, to live the present moment with consciousness and free of projections from the past.

A PATH TO SELF

AIC is used with people who cannot speak as well as those who can. The vision of handicap undergoes a quantum shift. The typed texts show that, no matter what the handicap is that limits communication or speaking, an intact conscience unfolds at another level of reality than the cognitive or sensorial system.

The support of the hand opens the access to this intact part of the individual. It is an approach that seems simple, yet requires that the professionals using it be in a very special state of presence.

It is a state of consciousness that allies vigilance and total release, which allows the sacred aspect of the text to emerge.

More than with other therapeutic approaches, the therapist's posture must be impeccable to guarantee the quality of the session.

An attitude of "savior" by the therapist would provoke an instability which would negatively influence the quality, and the vibrational frequency, of the text emerging via the Accompanied Inner Communication.

The risk of projection would also be increased. In this sense, it is like the image of a tightrope walker.

When I work, my heart is connected in its sacred dimension as well as with the person being accompanied; I am fully present at that instant, free of all anticipation.

AIC was developed as a direct result of my life's path.

A PATH TO SELF

It prepared me to constantly enlarge my belief system for the benefit of a vision of the human being that integrates various representations of the world and life.

Here is a brief description of the essential steps that prepared me to develop and practice Accompanied Inner Communication.
I was born in Uruguay and I lived in Argentina for the first four years where my father was working. I learned French and Spanish simultaneously.
I don't remember too much about that period, but my parents often described my agility to juggle from one language to another often acting as interpreter for my playmates.
A disastrous professional situation forced my parents to leave Argentina rapidly and return to France. I lost all of my bearings.
Whenever my parents spoke to me in Spanish I would answer in French, until my parents were so fed up that they stopped. So, I rapidly forgot Spanish, maybe as a way of fitting in.
I have always been fascinated by the mystery of words, so different from one language to another, yet reflecting the same reality.
I studied German, specializing in linguistics before teaching for a few years.
Meeting the man who was to become my husband propelled me into another universe.
He was working in Dubai, and I went to live with him there. We lived in the village of Kafji, Saudi Arabia near the Kuwaiti border, for almost two years.
I started to learn Arabic and refused the recluse-like life recommended for European women.

A PATH TO SELF

Because women were not allowed to drive cars, I bought myself a bicycle to travel in the area. The Saudi women opened their arms and hearts warmly which allowed me to discover another world. Once again, I had to let go of my traditional references.

Years later, after returning to France and then a brief stay in Singapore, we settled down in Japan with three young children. I lived the first few months in Tokyo as if I had been totally uprooted. Never had my personal/life references been so shaken.

The fundamental values that I based my life on - even in Saudi Arabia - were eaten away like a wood beam eaten by termites. In the beginning the country seemed cruel, until I realized that the social cohesion was based on values radically different than those in Judeo-Christian cultures.

In order to feel less isolated, I made the necessary adjustments to become integrated in the neighborhood community where we lived; from then on, I realized I could count on unfailing support.

I spent long hours committed to learning the spoken and written language. Little by little I integrated another way of functioning. With ideograms I discovered another access to language. An ideogram contains a quantity of information. The word is no longer linear; it becomes a sphere rich with symbolic contents.

The adoption of our fourth child, a little girl of Korean origin, was a big step on my personal path to the conscience of the human being part of ONE – disregarding cultures – ONE where the binding element is LOVE.

A PATH TO SELF

Today, I understand how all of these different cultural environments prepared me for my current activity: Accompanied Inner Communication.

While we were living abroad, I taught whenever it was possible. After returning to France, I quickly felt stifled teaching in the local high school. So, I decided to make a career change and study to become a psychotherapist.

My meeting with Pierre Weil was a decisive element that nudged me towards the transpersonal dimension of psychotherapeutic care. What I learned during the courses he taught was an important milestone for Accompanied Inner Communication. This encounter helped me put into words my personal inner experiences and to contact a sacred area that I had always felt but had not cultivated.

Beyond the important events in our lives and their influences, an unhurt conscience exists in the heart of our being which dilates with each experience that life allows us to traverse. Accompanied Inner Communication reveals this aspect of our being which grows as we transform to integrate the more or less painful experiences that punctuate our path.

Chapter 1

Encounter with transpersonal psychology

It seems to me that the approach I use daily in my accompaniment has existed since the beginning of time. Very young children, so receptive to their family and friends, have the capacity to catch what emerges from each person's heart. But, the capacity to put it into words, to express the feeling, is not yet available to the child and the family might not understand what is being felt in the intimacy of the young person concerned.

Most of us progressively lose this sharp perception of the other's life. It was a long process for me to regain this ability consciously. This ability only manifests itself in specific situations, as in helping others and above all when serving those unable to speak. Everything leads me to believe that it is relative to the emergence of a potential that we are progressively reconnecting with today.

A PATH TO SELF

As with each time a new possibility opens up for mankind, inner communication has emerged in different places, in different ways. I met a mother who had an essential need to communicate with her child who was unable to speak, and so with no previous training she spontaneously communicated with him thanks to "accompanied writing" by cupping his hand.

My own path was more laborious and three meetings were essential to the pathway that has become mine today.

This route is located at the convergence of three meetings, all fundamental to the direction that was mine. Accompanied Inner Communication was born where three distinct however complimentary rivers meet.

Chronologically my first decisive encounter with transpersonal psychology was with Pierre Weil the pioneer of this approach in France. My understanding of Facilitated Communication and then thorough training in Family Constellations allowed me to put in place what is called today Accompanied Inner Communication.

The encounter of transpersonal psychology through the intermediary of Pierre Weil propelled me into a field I had known since I was a child, but was not able to give it a name.

As far back as I can remember, and independent of all religious training, I had always had the intimate conviction that my body was like a piece of clothing; and that there was something bigger and more conscious that pre-existed it.

When I was about four or five years old, I would frequently pinch my arm to see what happened to my skin and also what I felt.

I observed my body and asked myself to what extent was it really real.

I looked in the mirror with this question: Why am I white and not black, why am I here in this country, in this family?

In the middle of all of these questions rushing around in my mind, this one came back incessantly: Why would Jesus be more divine than Buddha or Mohammed?

During my adolescence, I was inhabited by the idea that God manifested differently, in different places, at different times in history, and each time he chose the most appropriate type of manifestation. However, my inner conviction of a "higher power" always left me with an uneasy feeling.

Another question was always present: Is God only transcendent and therefore in a certain way, exterior to man?

If he is everywhere as I had been taught, then how can he be exterior?

What corresponds to this aspect of myself that I feel the existence of and that manifests itself sometimes during inner experiences?

What is the Soul and how does it manifest its divine nature? When I was 20 years old, I became interested in yoga and started reading everything I could get my hands on, looking for an answer.

A PATH TO SELF

I Lived in Japan for several years. In that country, what we call today shamanism[1] has remained alive in the form of Shintoism. My encounter with the Japanese culture initiated me to the representation of an imminent God present in all forms of life. Shintoism venerates the spirit of life in men but also in rocks, rivers and all forms of life. Ah! Maybe I had found a possible answer to my inner question. If God is both transcendent and immanent, he is both interior and exterior. Therefore that divine spark that I feel inside of me could correspond to this aspect of inner God that is in all forms of life. Little by little reading various books helped me define my own representation.

The books that had a large impact on my personal path were from various sources: but essentially the internationally known writers: C.G. Jung, Marie Louise von Franz[2], Satprem[3], *"Mind of the Cells: Or Willed Mutation of Our Species"*, *"Mother Or the Divine Materialism"* and *Sri Aurobindo, or the Adventure of Consciousness* and finally "Dialogues with an Angel" [4] retranscribed by Gitta Mallasz which was a revelation to me.

Pierre Weill's teachings helped me unify the awareness that punctuated my existence and integrate the transformations of my references after fifteen years in Asia. The description of transpersonal psychology will be detailed in a later chapter.

Here is a brief glimpse: The transpersonal domain gives access to a space beyond personal experience and corresponds to an increase in conscience, which opens a connection with the transcendent dimension of each person.

This field immediately places the individual in a larger context that includes him and contains him. The family is a "container" that acts as a base and support throughout every human life. This framework is the first in a series of helping elements, that are like Russian dolls, one fitting inside of the other, where each one has an impact on the life of the individual in the center.

The family is an integral part of a sociocultural context that inscribes itself in the historical and geographical context of one or more countries.

I was trained by Pierre Weil to teach his course "The art of living in peace". Prior to that, I had followed all of his courses called "The art of living life." Pierre Weil was one of the pioneers of transpersonal psychology. What I learned during my training with him allowed me to understand the meaning of the inner experiences that were difficult for me to share. It also gave me the impetus I needed to accompany others while respecting their sacred dimension.

From my point of view, transpersonal psychotherapy is similar to accompanying someone on their evolutionary path, and that is exactly what Accompanied Inner Communication allows.

A PATH TO SELF

Here are a few key details about Pierre Weil: Born the 16th of April 1924 in Strasbourg, France into a family with three conflicting religions and two opposing cultures; French and German. This context contributed to Pierre Weil becoming someone "Looking for Peace." When he was fourteen years old he wrote in his diary: *"My homeland is not only France, it is especially the Earth"*. He died October 10, 2008 in Brasilia.

After studying with famous educators and psychologists, he graduated from the French University Paris IV with a doctorate in psychology.

After studying psychotherapy he became chair in social psychology at the Federal University of Belo Horizonte (Brazil). At the end of his career he was chair in transpersonal psychology for which he was one of the pioneers in the worl

Increasingly successful in his life, he ended up with an existential crisis, cancer and the loss of his reason for living. He then started asking himself essential questions about the meaning of life and death. This questioning guided him to find answers in a synthesis between the Orient and Western cultures and between yoga and psychoanalysis. He was twenty years ahead of the UNESCO Declaration of Venise which recommends the complimentary encounter between the left brain and the right brain, between the West and the Orient. During this research, he met yoga masters like Swami Chinanda, Muktananda and Tibetan lamas such as Kanjur Rimpoché and Pemala Rimpoché.

A PATH TO SELF

The founding of the Peace University in Brasilia: In 1986 he was invited by the Governor of Brasilia to create the Foundation City of Peace. He was elected President and his function was to create and manage the International University of Brasilia, Unipaz.

In 1988, Pierre Weil elaborated a theory about the genesis of the destruction of life on the planet and the principles and approaches permitting a new way of educating for Peace. In Brasilia, he created a University for Peace as well as a kindergarten where 250 children live together in harmony and learn to live every day with peace in their hearts.

His work on Peace and the conscience was presented to UNESCO and its General Director Federico Mayor. Since1991, this work has been published in six languages. In 2000 he received an honorable mention for the UNESCO Prize for Peace Education.

Pierre Weil managed to integrate in most of his educational programs this integrative trilogy of the three aspects of Peace:

1. Peace with oneself (Ecology and Individual Conscience), concerned with the body, emotions and spirit.
2. Peace with others (Ecology and Social conscience), concerned with the economy, society and politics, and culture.
3. Peace with Nature (Ecology and the conscience of the Universe), concerned with matter, life and information. [2]

A PATH TO SELF

The imprint of Pierre Weil's instruction on my training courses:

Four of Pierre Weil's points particularly impressed me:

The first concerns the words "My homeland is not only France, it is especially the Earth". My personal route helped me understand that I too am a "citizen of the world". With Pierre Weil I found a "vastness" that dissolves limits and invites one to constantly challenge ones belief system. It is also what my encounters with cultures so different from ours, like the Japanese culture, invited me to challenge.
The goal of the Accompanied Inner Communication training I have organized is to open future accompanying therapists to an integrative vision of the world and life, by questioning belief systems that are above all references, different from one culture to another, yet complimentary.
Accompanying another person on his evolutionary path implies never stopping on one's own path. The accompanier should also be on his own path. From my point of view, reevaluating one's beliefs is unavoidable ethically and evolutionarily.

The second point relates to the synthesis that Pierre Weil made between the West and the Orient, between practicing yoga and psychoanalysis. C.G.Jung's book « The Psychology of Kundalini Yoga" has this same goal of connecting two keys to understanding to highlight their complementarity. I conscientiously practiced yoga for years while in Asia and felt deeply nourished by the Paul Weil's synthesis which integrates and unites these two visions of the world.

In my training courses, I use this understanding that takes into account the way the consciousness increases. This is done on two planes:

On the horizontal plane, the expansion of the conscience allows the integration of different aspects of the being and the personal experiences to unify; the person does not feel divided, mental silence settles in little by little.

And on the vertical plane, which relates to the progression of the psychic energy in the energetic centers with the consequence of erasing the egotic preoccupations benefitting more universal preoccupations.

The third point is inspired by Pierre Weill and his meeting with Tibetan lamas.
It concerns the viewpoint that attachment is a source of suffering. According to Pierre Weil, a particular form of attachment, which slows evolution, connects with each energy center. This attachment is responsible for the pleasure received when reaching certain objectives and the fear of losing the desired object.

A PATH TO SELF

Fear has three aspects:
>   fear of not obtaining what we want
>   fear of losing what we obtained
>   fear of not finding what we lost

Our attachment creates a fixation which can hinder our evolution. This fixation is then the cause of our discomfort because of what the fear of losing implies: for example concerning the attachment to money, being loved, a social status, etc.

Compulsive repetitions are found at this level encouraging a vicious circle in which causes and effects follow each other, creating repetitive patterns.
We are in the presence of a closed system where the evolutionary process is blocked. The ego tends to settle itself at the chakra where the repetitive patterns are established (it finds a certain security).

The fourth point, which is essential, is linked to the understanding that our outer life experiences are the mirror of what happens inside of us. Therefore, for peace to establish itself on Earth, it must first reign in our own heart.
One of the objectives of AIC is precisely to help the person who has come to be accompanied welcome each life experience with a Yes to life.

And as one accompanied person wrote: *"integrate myself with flexibility in the flow of life, welcome all without refusing anything. Welcome gift of life to be other than what was foreseen by expectant waiting."* This yes to what life presents generates inner peace.

After participating in Michael Roads[3] seminars for ten years, I can also say that he has imprinted the way I undertake my work as accompanier. His viewpoint on life invites us to constantly enlarge our belief system conscious of the limitations we impose upon ourselves. I am not going to go into detail because the contents would exceed the objectives of this book. However, a short essential sentence summarizes the focal point of his message "Choose Love". This short sentence is also a connecting thread regarding our posture as accompanier and refers first of all, to our relationship with ourselves, a vast program....

Before going more into detail concerning the objectives of our work, I would like to share with you the second encounter that was essential for the elaboration of Accompanied Inner Communication. It was Facilitated Communication.

A PATH TO SELF

Chapitre 2

Encounter with Facilitated Communication

As I was preparing to leave teaching, little by little I trained to help children in difficulty. The work of "emotional grammar" and the expression of emotions by Isabelle Filliozat opened new doors for me.

The training in "Waking Dream Therapy" with Georges Romey and also a cure of Waking Dreams connected me to the power of symbols which I had previously felt in *my work with ideograms.*

To begin with, all of these efforts, which helped me progress with consciousness and to get to know myself better, were motivated by my desire to help children with difficulties at school. The drive was that of a motivated teacher: how is it that intelligent children are blocked to learning? How can we adults help them realize their potential to the fullest?

A friend spoke to me about an article in the "Le Monde" newspaper describing Facilitated Communication. My first reaction was: wow, what a fantastic discovery, but it is not for me, I have no predisposition for that type of work. My friend participated in the first phase of training, and came back enthusiastic.

My resistances were surreptitiously damaged. The same friend suggested I act as one of her "guinea pigs" thus experiencing the process from the inside.

I became more and more troubled however without forgetting my primary goal: helping children release their blocks to freely access education. Maybe this tool would help me identify the blocks?

Finally, I decided to sign up for the training program.

Facilitated Communication, FC:

This approach was developed by Rosemary Crosley in several countries particularly in

Australia. She trained the speech therapist who transmitted this technique to me.

FC calls on conscious communication and is primarily for people who cannot speak and is often used to help them make choices in their everyday life and acquire knowledge.

It is an alternative method of communication.

At Syracuse University in the USA, there is a training course in "Facilitated Communication."

In Germany, the technique is called "Gestützte Kommunikation," which means assisted or helped communication, and designates this same form of communication.

No matter which words are used, this type of communication is primarily used as an alternative for non-speaking people, no matter what their handicap is.

The objective is to help the person in question become as much as possible, the center of his life thanks to conscious choices thusly facilitated and in some cases acquiring total written autonomy.

It is possible to make pictograms and help the movements of the handicapped person to overcome neuromotor difficulties and allow the gesture to be complete.

After pre-learning the alphabet using pictograms (representing the letters in the alphabet) it is sometimes possible to acquire typing autonomy. Of course this autonomy is uncertain and depends on the person's handicap.

Practically speaking: as an "accompanier" who supports the hand of the person writing, I sit next to the person and make sure that our chairs are parallel so as to avoid any torsion of the shoulders. The right hand is open facing upwards to the sky, with a cupping motion. I welcome the person's left hand in my palm with my fingers folded back except for the index.
His index is isolated and ready to push the keys on the computer keyboard in front of us. I take the necessary time to center myself and "listen" to my partner's hand. This means that I put myself in a state of receptivity to perceive the beginning of movement.
After a few seconds, I feel an impulsion coming from his hand. The movement that I accompany is thus initiated. My partner's hand takes me to the keys on the keyboard and words are formed.

Concerning terminology, and to simplify understanding for further reading, we will use the vocabulary from FC and refer to the facilitator as the person cupping the hand, and facilitated, the person who is being accompanied.
The hypothesis developed by the neurologist John Eccles[4] in which "The unity of the conscience or the soul comes from an entity located in another level of reality," sheds light on what might happen/be happening during the facilitation process.

Accepting the consequences of such a hypothesis allows many handicapped people to benefit from facilitated communication, without taking into consideration evolution towards possible autonomy.

Actually, no matter what the state of the accompanied person's brain, the facilitator acts as a motor, sensorial and cognitive moderator, which means he "lends" his "communication tools" to his partner.

John Eccles' hypothesis implies that any person, no matter what their handicap is, disposes of an intact conscience which deploys itself at a different level of reality than the cognitive and sensorial system.

By making himself available to the person he is facilitating, the facilitator becomes the communication partner's conscious receptor.

He can thus express himself using the brain of his facilitator, which will compensate the deficiencies of his own sensorial and cognitive possibilities.

Therefore, the person I facilitate, benefits from my own vocabulary and my mental structures, made available via the hand I support.

Such a hypothesis is totally in harmony with my own personal experiences.

It is also confirmed by the teachings of all the large well known spiritual traditions as well as the transpersonal psychology teaching, and by Pierre Weil's experiences.

The texts typed by non speaking people have a profound impact on their family, testifying to wisdom and a depth seemingly incompatible with the person's exterior. Thanks to AIC the limits of appearance are transcended and the person finally has the right to be quoted.

Here is a text by Muriel, an adult suffering from autistic disorders, describing a reality she has access to:

"Sky's light blooms into a bronze colored rainbow where I see the range of colors fan out over the space of time. I live in osmosis with the world and it is joy to open a crack to learn to be me. My fear is left on deposit on the mirror of my life.

"My life reflects on the mirror of your thought, like an image in a mirror. Head on is not my way. I attack myself rather than the other who is also me and I refer to my feeling of insufficiency. However, deep down, I know that the Whole is in me and that I am an integral part of the Whole (..) autism is not irrationality, but rationality so big that the world seems without sense."

What do we really know about what is lived "consciously" by these people? Where does Facilitated Communication stop and where does Inner Communication begin? Also, maybe the people who cannot speak live constantly in this transpersonal environment? Extremely receptive to what their family and relations live, open to truths that go beyond the conscience of people referred to as "normal."

The depth of their writing is unquestionable and in keeping with the hypothesis that life experiences exceed personal experiences.

Pierre Weil's path nourished the evolution that contributed to the elaboration of Accompanied Inner Communication.

From Facilitated Communication to Accompanied Inner Communication (AIC):

Accompanied Inner Communication is related to a transpersonal type of communication by the fact that there is an expansion of the conscience during the session.

The accompaniment with Accompanied Inner Communication, allows the person accompanied to progressively leave a sensation of being fragmented from repressed wounds, to consciously find a feeling of unity.
Therefore, during an AIC session, the access to a state of transpersonal conscience permits the feeling that reality is not lived like a duel.

Painful memories emerge from the unconscious and are integrated in a conscience that grows with each session.

From an Asian interpretative viewpoint, the palm of the hand is an additional center for the heart's energy.

A PATH TO SELF

We can interpret supporting the hand as a posture that connects the person accompanying and the person being accompanied, heart to heart.

This way of accompanying contributes to establishing contact with what I refer to as the accompanied person's « center of truth » and from this center, welcoming and integrating all of the hidden or sometimes disassociated aspects of the personality.

The goal is to allow a unification process of one's being and expand one's conscience with recognition and acceptation of all of the aspects of the person's being; reconciling opposites within the conscience.

This is the way reconciliation occurs in the individual, ending the confrontation thus allowing inner peace to take root, little by little.

Via the typed text, one of the objectives of AIC is to allow the accompanied person to become more conscious of himself, releasing his attachment with the past and his fear of the future, thus learning how to live the present moment consciously.

Another essential aspect of AIC is the accompaniment. This takes place on two levels:

A PATH TO SELF

- Firstly, from a gestural point of view, because accompanying the gesture gives access to the computer keyboard.
- Secondly, from a psychological point of view. The person accompanying is like a well-meaning witness, who welcomes what is typed.
He is also there to provide a safe area that the accompanied person did not previously have; leaving him feeling overwhelmed and alone.
The goal is that the person can slowly integrate, bit by bit, the unacknowledged aspects of his psychic whole.

We will go into more detail about Accompanied Inner Communication in the following chapters.
Now I would like to present the third meeting that was decisive for the elaboration of AIC.

A PATH TO SELF

Chapter 3

My meeting with Constanze Lang and Family Constellations

During Accompanied Inner Communication sessions, it is very common that what is typed via the cupped hand describes a past transgenerational experience.

Thus, the life experience of a deceased ancestor can be brought to light and can help the accompanied person understand his repetitive behaviors or certain unexplained emotions he feels regularly. As though an ancestor was speaking through his descendant's life, expressing the tonality of his unresolved conflicts.

The transmission of our family's history is certainly part of us from our very young age.

A PATH TO SELF

Even if a baby does not speak, he perceives what precedes language; he « catches or hears » both parents' subconscious. And they in turn are influenced by their families' predecessors.

To be able to better understand the mechanisms of this transmission, I studied Family Constellations for several years with Constanze Lang[5]. The type of Family Constellation training I received from Constanze Lang was initiated by Bert Hellinger[6].
The method he perfected consists of family members being represented by volunteers in a given space, and then observing the evolution of their dynamics.

The expression « Family Constellation » comes from the German word «Familienaufstellung», and the literal translation is "family placing or positioning".

The two most significant ancestors of Family Constellations are:

- On one hand, Virginia Satir[7] a specialist in family relationships, family therapy, self esteem and communication. She was one of the first psychotherapists to enlarge her field of work to the heart dimension, self-love and to identify everyone's hope for inner peace. She used to say, « I love to see my patients leave with stars in their eyes ».

- And on the other hand, Jacob-Lévy Moréno[8], who invented psychodrama and had the idea of using a group as a transforming agent. Moreno put his patients on a theater stage and invited them to a "catharsis" of their emotions, playing improvised roles in front of spectators, to help regain their balance thus liberating their relational or affective blocks. The action of the psychodrama allows switching roles from those the patient is locked into, thus rediscovering creative resources.

Everything is connected in an imperceptible way. Pierre Weil whose training was very decisive for me, also met J-L Moréno and worked with him to later develop what he refers to as cosmodrama, like "a tri-dimensional model that connected states of conscience with inner and outer realities."

Progressively, I integrated the approach of Family Constellations in my own therapeutic work. Family Constellations and Accompanied Inner Communication aim for the same goal. Thanks to the typed text, the objective of AIC is to allow ourselves to become more conscious of ourselves, release our attachment to the past, and our fear of the future, thus learning to consciously live in the present, consciously.
In this way, step by step, we leave a situation of helplessness, in which we feel we are victims, to become responsible of our own future and independent.

The family positioning using figurines visually enhances what is written.

These two techniques are very complimentary and my experience has shown how much their combined use can multiply the efficiency of the therapy.

What emerges during a Constellation reflects a family's unconscious, whereas Accompanied Inner Communication allows access to the accompanied person's unconscious, which also includes - among other things – the family unconscious.
Therefore, these two techniques complete each other and each contributes to the well being of the accompanied person.

Being able to see what is « playing » in the « generational movie » helps de-dramatize the events lived in our childhood. The past is not modified; it is our inner vision that is transformed. What was unacceptable becomes understandable.

Looking back on the past gives meaning to the difficulties we experienced and anchors us in the present.

How a Family Constellation is conducted:

The Family Constellation work takes place within a group of at least twelve people with a leader trained in this technique.

The objective is to clarify a specific challenge or issue. Pure curiosity by a client regarding his family is in no way accepted for a Family Constellation.

A PATH TO SELF

The workshop's participants sit in a large circle and the constellation takes place inside this circle. The person (the client) seeking to understand an issue sits next to the leader. To begin with, the challenge or question is clarified with the client.

The challenge could be something like « I have a conflicting relationship with my eldest son and I don't understand what is happening between us". Or: «Everything is fine in my life but sometimes I feel overwhelmed by a deep sadness I do not understand ».

The leader asks a few factual questions. In function of the family story and the challenge described, the facilitator will say which family members he thinks are necessary to place at the beginning of the Family Constellation.

Then, the client will choose among the members of the group, those who will represent the selected members of his family and also someone to represent himself/herself. During the Family Constellation, the facilitator may integrate other family member representatives, as needed.

The leader then asks the client to place the family representatives as he/she feels to be correct, in function of their relationship. This positioning is done instinctively, without thinking. An energy field is thus created between the representatives.

From what the representatives feel and express out loud, the challenges we live are seen more clearly. Their movements express the elements that want to be liberated, progressing towards a resolution.

The constellation leader is attentive to everything that weakens or strengthens the family representatives that have been positioned.

This principle is the guideline for all of the leader's work and he/she favors the interventions that render the representatives stronger.

Symbolic sentences are suggested with the goal of putting into words and consciously integrating the resolution of the constellation and the new order established.

They are very simple sentences that are addressed to the soul. They correspond only to the situation at that moment and are the fruit of a respectful attitude towards the people concerned.

Someone who lost his/her mother at birth might say:
« I accept my life at the price it cost you and what it cost me and I will do something good in memory of you."
    Or:
« It has been very hard, you gave me life, and I will do something good with it. »

At the end of the constellation, each representative leaves or "steps outside" of his/her role consciously, to return to their own identity.

A PATH TO SELF

In a private session: It is possible to use the constellation principle in an individual session. Personally, I use wooden figurines to replace the representatives.

This work which is very complementary to Accompanied Inner Communication helps create fluid communications within a family. The objective of this work is to clarify a specific issue.

During this work, the energies that were blocking the family system will be liberated. They are available so that the unconscious can use them differently with the benevolence and blessings of the ancestors with whom we are connected.

The story has not changed, but our view on it has been modified. So, the memory is transformed.

Common denominators between AIC and Family Constellations:

The therapist's attitude is almost identical. In both cases:

- I am present in the now with a floating-like attention.
- I trust the process and allow myself to be guided by what comes.
- I remain centered and aligned with my heart.
- I have no intentions; the intention to heal is not one of my objectives.

I am merely present and in harmony with what emerges.

Experience has shown that if I want to help someone and it helps me to help, then the other person is weakened by my intention. It is impossible to know what is right for the other.

Regarding Accompanied Inner Communication, the facilitator is a benevolent witness, who welcomes and accompanies what is typed, by his presence.

- I am only a mediator
- I am conscious that the forces at work in the process are beyond the individual.

When I facilitate Accompanied Inner Communication, I am within an space similar to that of the Constellations.

As a family representative in a constellation, I have the physical sensations, emotions and the types of relationships of the people being represented.

When accompanying with AIC, I am also in contact with inner experiences of the person being accompanied. I share his/her energy field. In German we speak of « wissende Feld », which can be translated by "field that knows". It is a field bearing information about the systems and the individuals.

The sentences that are expressed during a Family Constellation session, are in conformity with what emanates from the energy field that encompasses the representatives. The leader is in tune with this

field and expresses what he/she feels. They are in harmony with the soul's vibration. Therefore, they are correct. Words have a specific "weight" or power and each word is important.
Each word must be very carefully chosen because the energy within the group is intense and the work profound.

The importance of each word is also found in the AIC work. Sometimes, the hand remains poised in the air over the keyboard until the appropriate word emerges.

With both techniques, the person accompanying or facilitating, needs to clear his/her mind to welcome what is manifested, with no preconceptions –for the typed texts or when observing what happens in the constellation.

In my work with Accompanied Inner Communication, I take into account the person who comes to see me, but also his family and social context.
His uneasiness cannot be separated from the family and social interactions in which he expresses himself.

This overall understanding of the person is of course important during the discussion preceding the first session. I ask questions about the family make-up and dramatic events that happened in his life. But, I do not spend a lot of time with questions and avoid all types of judgments by my client regarding his family. We calmly get to the facts.

A PATH TO SELF

The person describes his issue, and the session can begin.

As unusual as they may seem, neither of the two types of therapy I have discussed call for any type of « magic » capable of resolving the issue that the person has come to see us for in a few sessions. For the session to be effective, it is essential that the client claim as his own, the changes initiated during the session.

After a family constellation, the client's conscience will allow him to meet his family members from a healing perspective, in conformity with what appeared during the constellation. This also includes the inner contact established when thinking of the people concerned.

In the same way, what emerges in AIC can only be totally active if the person concerned takes responsibility for the changes which began during the session. A conscious path is initiated; it is the path of an entire life. In both Accompanied Inner Communication and Family Constellations, the facilitator is simply a mediator, facilitating transformation.

Curiosity regarding a family event has no place in the AIC process nor in the Family Constellations. The objective is not to go digging in one's past, but rather to let what is useful from the past express itself as needed during the session

The constellation will help the person release a specific obstacle that was stopping him/her from advancing. It will also allow him to live his own destiny in accordance with his life.

The text written in Accompanied Inner Communication will let parts of the past express themselves as needed to live the present with a heightened conscience. This will allow the accompanied person to find harmony in his everyday life and to communicate smoothly with those who share his life.

Via the typed text, the accompanied person can become more conscious of himself/herself, release attachment with the past and his/her fear of the future so as to live each instant, consciously.

The objective of being accompanied either with AIC or with a constellation, is also to allow each person to leave their position as victim, become responsible of their future and independent.
 A session has the effect of « verticalizing » or "helping the person stand up for himself" and regain the autonomy needed to slowly leave his patterns of dependency.

In the case of accompanying people unable to speak, the situation seems reversed.
Most of the time, a handicap goes hand in hand with a rich inexpressible inner experience. The person, who is unable to verbally communicate, is actually in connection with everything alive around him or her.
Accompanied Inner Communication will give this person the possibility to express his/her inner wealth and to take his/her place in the world.

A PATH TO SELF

It will also allow him to structure himself interiorly with the consciousness of time as distinctly past, present and future, even though they are connected.

Accompanied Inner Communication, which I could also call, communication of the heart, was given to humanity by people unable to speak. Speech, which allows interaction between individuals, could at first be considered a separating element before becoming understood as a reuniting element, thanks to relationships.

A baby is like a sponge; in osmosis with its family and surroundings. Words will progressively give him/her the understanding of his specific identity, separate from his mother, father and surroundings. With speech, the child enters the personal field.

People, who cannot verbally express themselves because of their handicap, remain in contact with the field that goes beyond the person.

Accompanied Inner Communication is specific in that it allows the expression of experiences that transcend the person. This one fact places it in the field of transpersonal approaches.

The next chapter will hopefully clarify this terminology to include Accompanied Inner Communication.

Chapter 4

AIC and Transpersonal Psychology

Birth and fields of investigation in transpersonal psychology:

Transpersonal psychology integrates the spiritual dimension in psychology and psychotherapy, following in C.G.Jung's footsteps. The term « transpersonal » was used for the first time by C.G.Jung in an article from 1917 titled: "The Personal and the Collective, or Transpersonal Unconscious". Jung distinguished three levels:

The conscience – The personal unconscious (content forgotten or repressed, sensitive perceptions that never attained the conscious however they had penetrated the psyche) and the collective unconscious, which is not individual but common to human beings. Jung explained that the unconscious that regroups all of the archetypes, is the depository of everything that humanity has lived – going back to its most obscure beginnings, not as a dead depository, like a field of abandoned ruins, but rather a system of reactions and availabilities that determine individual life. The processes of the collective unconscious are often represented as natural elements like the ocean or the forest, but also the archetype of the Grandmother or the Soul.

Literally, the term « transpersonal » means beyond the personal, beyond the personality. It consists in recognizing that what we are is not limited to our personality.

Beyond the ego, beyond the body, we can follow our route on paths that have been described in several spiritual traditions. In the 60's, Abraham Maslow[9], Stanislav Grof[10] and Antony Sutich[11] used the term transpersonal to describe a new branch of psychology which integrated their understanding of the oriental mystical traditions in relation to the humanist psychology of which they were the figureheads.

With his doctoral thesis, « The sphinx, mystery and structure of man » presented at the French University-Paris VII, Pierre Weill introduced transpersonal psychology in France during the 70's.

A PATH TO SELF

According to Abraham Maslow, transpersonal psychology should be considered as a fourth force in the field of psychology.

- The first is the psychology of the depths, described by Freud and which speaks of motivation, psychodynamics and mental pathology mostly through case studies.
- The second is behaviorism which studies learning, conditioned and observable behavior stressing experimental methods.
- The third is humanist psychology which is mainly concerned by the human condition, emotions, attitudes and therapy. The human is considered as free, unique and responsible. He is capable of assuming his choices. The limit of this practice is the exclusion of the spiritual dimension.
- The fourth, transpersonal psychology, considers that the human being is not reduced to mental and material mechanics but is fundamentally defined as a spiritual essence. It also studies the states encountered by humans beyond everyday life.

Its objective is also to facilitate increased consciousness by the integration of everything that was lived by the individual during his lifetime, allowing him to return to unity, consciously.

The states of modified consciousness are obtained through meditation, dreams, spiritual experiences and connect man with his divine essence.

A PATH TO SELF

Regarding Transpersonal Psychology, each person carries within himself a sacred potential of wisdom, love and creativity. The full realization of this potential of divine essence that resides in the depths of the unconscious is the objective of an evolutionary path. This goes together with the new concept of the unconscious that is neither reduced neither to Freud's repression nor to the biological organism.

One of the characteristics of transpersonal psychology is to include in one same inner movement, states of consciousness that are usually disassociated.

A sharp yet tranquil vigilance which corresponds in the brain to beta waves, with a rather rapid frequency, is associated with non-focused attention, available and totally receptive. In this case, we notice slower frequency alpha waves in the brain.

The specificity of the transpersonal state is the merging of these two states: corresponding to a state of wakefulness and dreaming, and their integration in a unified movement of the conscience.

A PATH TO SELF

Accompanied Inner Communication : a transpersonal approach

- ### Posture of the accompanier in relation to the solicited states of conscience

The access to an inexpressible experience by conscious speech is facilitated by the modified state of consciousness of the accompanier and the person being accompanied, during a session of Accompanied Inner Communication.

Even though AIC seems in principle to be easy, it demands that the professional use a very particular state of presence combining vigilance and a totally relaxed state, respectful of the sacredness of the emerging text.

The accompanier and the person being accompanied are united together in a field which gives them access to a modified state of consciousness.
The two states; wakefulness and expanded consciousness, are integrated in the process in one movement, which is in accordance with one of the specificities of transpersonal psychology.

As facilitator, I am vigilant, capable of having the necessary discernment required for all therapeutic accompaniments, while at the same time, extremely present in the moment in a state of consciousness close to what I can experience when meditating. Also, I have no memory of what was typed.

The therapist's correct posture is more important than with other types of therapy. It must be impeccable so as to guarantee the quality of the session. It is about balance, like a tightrope walker's posture. When I work, I am connected to my heart in its sacred dimension, as well as with that of the person I am accompanying. I am fully present in the moment, free from all anticipation.

- **Access to transcendence in everyone**

Actualizing this sacred potential, while releasing obstacles blocking fulfillment, is one of the main objectives of Accompanied Inner Communication.

The being reveals itself beyond words or rather via the words that emerge from the plenitude of each person's symbolic expression.

The process itself, thanks to the « heart to heart » contact guaranteed by accompanying the gesture of the hand, connects the person accompanied with his Essence.

Thanks to the meditation of the « accompanier », AIC facilitates communication by the « silent partner », welcoming without judging. During a session, the two protagonists are liberated of temporal constraints and the accompanying transformation takes place within this intangible silence which paces the breathing. It is the deep silence that exists between each of our thoughts, between each inhale and exhale, transcending space and time.

A PATH TO SELF

It is essential that the accompanier has previously embarked upon a process of self-unification and that at least during the session, he not lose contact with his own heart.   It is something like being connected to the Self *frequency*.

Therefore, the person whose hand I am cupping is automatically connected with his own frequency, at the level of his Self. It is as if I facilitated the personality to be in tune with the note of Self and vibrate in harmony with the soul's melody.

I see myself as a simple mediator enabling the essential note of the *Being* to be in phase, in tune, with that of the personality.

The people I accompany with Accompanied Inner Communication often relate feeling an experience that is almost « spiritual », what Jung called a numinous [12]experience.

The fact of reaching a deep reality that connects with the energy of life in its essential form is in itself a source of profound transformation for the person experiencing it.

However, before the Self shows itself completely, one must take off or rather integrate via transformation, the numerous veils that hide it. We have to consciously look at our attachments, our conditioning. We need to bandage our childhood and adult wounds, and take into consideration our unconscious loyalties to family patterns. Finally, little by little, we dare let go of our appearances: to reach the essence and express our uniqueness, beyond masks and appropriateness.

- **Integration of the disassociated aspects of the psyche**

Becoming the Being we truly are, implies slowly integrating all of the aspects of our personality that were until then disassociated from our unifying center, or center of truth, and were leading their own lives.

These disassociated parts push us to accomplish acts that another aspect of ourselves, disapproves. We feel divided and don't know how to access inner peace that we profoundly desire. Slowly, without judgment, we need to recognize these different aspects of ourselves and accept that they coexist within us without fighting amongst themselves.

Accompanied Inner Communication permits this integration of the different aspects of our personality. The transformation of what is brought to light starts during a session and the inner work continues its action for several days.

The aspects of the personality that could not be accepted by the conscience emerge bit by bit and are transformed through the words. Thusly, an adult describes his childhood with AIC:

« *Feeling of abandon, hidden sadness, mother involved, gone too far, mother betrayed, I feel rejected, humiliation concerns mother, coat of sadness covers her shoulders."*

And during the same session expresses:

« I release leaden weight that destroyed me; I uproot from my center this heavy weight of sadness. The child in me heals; path of reconciliation with myself liberates creative power. Inner sun blooms my heart's rose."

In my experience, the forgotten sufferings that are unveiled in the texts emerge only when the person is ready and able to receive them.

Like a mirror, the text reflects to the « accompanied person » the image of a painful experience, but it also allows him to come into contact with his inner force and build a foundation on which self-unification can take place.

This does not exempt the person concerned from personal inner work. Thanks to the personal work of accepting and integrating what emerges progressively, the conscience will enlarge its field, little by little.

In the same session, buried pain and hidden resources of the unconscious can be expressed and in a way, the AIC text acts as the unifying center of these opposite polarities.

It concerns harmonizing the opposites in oneself, integrating the unconscious in the conscious, so that the conscience expands and assimilates Self with a larger personality.

So, can Daniel who has difficulty putting himself forward especially being in public, find the strength he needs to re-connect with his inner strength? He is discreet and his job is not in accordance with his capabilities. He also tires easily, as if blocked from energy.

From the beginning of his text, he describes his intra-uterine life:
"Chill put in stomach's bag (he explained that his mother wore a girdle during her pregnancy), receiving of all my energy blocked. Terrified to leave comfortable swimming nest. I perceive life like storm to traverse." And a little farther: *"Joy to blow wind of peace on frenzied swimming. In me planted seed of confidence in life and myself."*

During the session after reading what he had typed, Daniel spoke of the fire that forced his mother, alone at home, to flee the family house quickly.

During the following session, he confirmed that the fire had taken place during the pregnancy. After this session, Daniel felt an enormous liberation.

- **Looking for meaning of Self**

Access to the depths of Self permits the expression of the unique and transcendental aspect present in each of us. What is said there also lets us reconnect with what makes our specificity.

The act of being put in contact with ones spiritual filiation, thanks to the cupping of the hand and the contents of the text, is very often en essential vector of growth, bearing an intrinsic meaning. Because of this, these lines were very helpful to Christine:

« Sweet feeling to reconnect with my true Self. The truth is beyond appearances. Nothing can touch nor damage that which is indescribable or indissoluble."

The people who come to see me are usually going through a difficult period.
Some, who had put all of their energy into social and professional success suddenly find themselves unemployed and without goals or motivation.

The departure of a spouse, a divorce, sudden bereavements, all of these can push people to ask existential questions. . Giving sense to these events helps release the pain and regain the indispensable life force.

Questions relative to the meaning of life affect all age groups and I am surprised by the maturity of young adults I meet today. Most are preoccupied with questions about their reasons for living. The texts written in AIC often have invaluable indications.

The sense is sometimes connected to the choice of activity that we are called to dedicate ourselves. The joy we procure is the infallible sign that indicates we are on the path that is right for us.

Corinne, who was one of my trainees going through a period of doubt concerning her activity as a psychotherapist, typed the following with my support:

« Soft unity in me makes its nest. I reconnect with all of my potentials and fairness to place my rocks of knowledge. Accompanying is a trump card, queen of diamonds gives me her support. Accompany humans on path of truth. Help each to find his right place in the game of life. (…)Connect myself to the other in his truth, queen is in me and pulls the strings."

One of Corinne's difficulties was with her acquaintances' reluctance relative to Accompanied Inner Communication which she had started learning. During the session, she gave herself the answer she needed:
« Different signals are possible; know how to manage attached circumstances is done little by little. Life line leads me towards my accomplishment. Realization obtained through helping relationships."

One should not consider AIC as a technique capable of answering all of the questions that arise. The goal of being accompanied is to permit the subject to find the answers by himself. The unconscious is wise enough not to systematically give all of the keys asked for. In certain circumstances only the part of the Self expressing itself in AIC will give the necessary help to the conscious part of the subject.

Most of the time, the person is referred to himself as in the following extract:
« Answers present in the heart of my heart. Make internal silent space and listen to voice of the heart."

Beyond the questions relating to our specific path, isn't the reason of our life to consciously find the Unity that presides All That Is.
Then, a lasting joy can take root, independent of the everyday trials and tribulations. Accompanied Inner Communication reconnects the person writing with his « Center of Truth ».
The values of Self impose themselves little by little and replace the demands of having. A conscious return to Unity begins and is amplified.
This return to unity is never completely explored. It opens to a rebirth, a new vision of the world thus beginning a totally different approach to daily life.

The following text, typed via Accompanied Inner Communication sheds light on the conscience that accompanies this rebirth:

« Life which is love and Light, transit through my incarnated being and nourishes the creative process of which I am the mediator and the creator of one piece. It is useful today to leave all space of separateness because life flows through you who is Me, Life flows through us, one and indivisible.

In the present incarnation which is yours today memory is obsolete, like a relic of a linear and dual way of functioning. You enter into the totality of spherical time and each instant brings the energy of the right act poised in the eternal present. And so life adopts the contours of the moment, life bursts forward and blossoms through your voice and your hands in the spontaneity of the right gesture."

The next chapter is dedicated to the accompaniment of people who cannot speak and will connect me directly with an unusual depth of expression and a sense of unity experienced daily.

Chapter 5

Accompanied Inner Communication serving people with special needs

Very quickly my attention is drawn to the content of texts that emerge with people unable to speak. There is a reoccurring specificity: these people feel what is lived far beyond their own lives.

This is manifested by a capacity to know what is happening to their family members and friends, even those living in another town or another area.

Geneviève, who cannot not speak any longer following a cerebrovascular accident, stays in contact with her grandchildren, and when I go see her to help her communicate, she gives advice to one and all. Via the keyboard the needs of each person are answered. She analyzes so subtly what is taking place far from her, that her written messages have a strong impact on those who receive them. This woman can maintain her function as grandmother thanks to the keyboard and also her correct place in the family constellation:

"I am staying a bit longer on Earth because I still feel useful to my grandchildren. They came to Earth in a world of disorder and their lives have a very particular meaning.

I honor their birth and I wish that each of them honors he who is above all that is visible. It is the privilege of my condition to see inside and above, I am a guide and this is my choice."

The consequences of this extreme receptivity affect everyday life. Geneviève picks up on the smallest conflict in the nursing team at the hospital. If there is a problem in her ward, the reorganization of the personnel would have an incidence on her quality of life because even negative thoughts go though the filter of her conscience.

"Tell (of my) great need to rest and find silence within self and also outside. There are disruptions that I pick up here, it is like chaos. Go tell the lady who does the cleaning in the morning to be quieter. Well, what I feel so strongly is in such contradiction with the total peace that settles in me more and more, that it is a distressing contrast, but that is the way it is, I accept.

I feel chaos, negative thought forms due to feelings between one another."

A PATH TO SELF

Concerning this inner "vastitude" or "immensity", Benoît, an adult suffering from autistic disorders, wrote in one of his first sessions with my colleague Marie Vialard-Hauser:

"Since my birth what I wanted to say is that the vibrations are enormous. The world is a universe that diffracts into fragments of truth; what I wanted to say is that the long chain of causes and effects is like a path without openings, is a closed room where we go around in circles; what I wanted to say Is there is a secret passage in the hearts of men and women in this world, there is a secret passage that opens to a larger world and I am a door opener I am a discoverer of these passages, I am Benoît who enlargens life. Life seems so small to me in your eyes and so immense in mine, sometimes much too big, too big, we only meet in the small parts of my truth. Sometimes, it is like I feel I am behind a wall and you go past me without seeing me, when you only see he who seems lost; I am lost each time I put myself in your view but if someone could see where I come from then I would still be connected to these luminous vibrations that could allow me to make adequate gestures and show the interest of my Being; but I chose not to have all of the words because I am only pure vibration; there is such a reduction with words; I wanted to show you that when I was small, I wanted to show you my world and you did not see it and it made me afraid to be almost the only one to see this world with such vibrations, infinite light in which I vibrate and so it is hard to

come back to Earth sometimes and how to say this and not seem to be crazier than autistic. "

His mother who was present during the session, told him something like *"words are part of the human condition, through them we communicate and pray"…*

Benoît answered: *"I accept the words of AIC because they are from the passage of the heart…."*

Timothée, a non-speaking trisomic adolescent who does not speak at all but who expresses himself with gestures, communicated via the keyboard – while moving around joyously:

"I say a new face is put on my own image, I tell you that these wise words give me a new face and if I move around the way I am, it is because it allows me to be opposite earthly reality without too many fears. I tell you that I move like a puppet when inside I behave, it is my path to deceive appearances so that appearances are consciously revisited."

He adds:

"Go see beyond, go see beyond what is written because what I write is beyond and words err with their incertitude, I say the words are good and soft and it is insufficient Yes, it is insufficient because my heart knows so much beyond what is seen outside and even with words of heart there are silences that we hear and others, silent silences

beyond words that no one hears yet are so strong with meaning.

Go seek the meaning in movement, it is time to see the meaning of my movements because they carry meaning of a vision of the world, mine and this vision is like a flying carpet, yes I am on my flying carpet and I go around the world looking for my profound identity, and these words from heart give an acute conscious to my identity even if that defies the barriers of what is visible."

What he expresses is similar with what Benoît said about the inadequacy of words to express inner experiences. Their texts bear witness to flawless integrity.

All of the texts by mute people are overwhelming and full of an immense desire to "live true" and to "speak true". The need of authenticity is essential in everyone. When one lives in the consciousness of Unity, nothing can be hidden, everything is perceived.

The depth of what is felt goes together with an obligation of integrity: *"worse to talk and say false words than to be quiet."*

The need for integrity concerns all sectors.

Alan wrote: *"Dirty is the road towards God, I am one of the chimney sweeps, humor allows changing way of looking: head down those who are proud are sheepish and the sheepish are proud. Flattening desire of victory flattens the man."*

A PATH TO SELF

Muriel evokes her feelings about love:

"Where is love? I see it in mommy's heart, I see it in your heart, I see it in the eyes of your cat. I see it where we don't always see it, because when it shows itself noisily, that means it is not."

The love that we are talking about starts with the acceptation of each person with his differences, without waiting. Anne-Christine types:

"First accept mute daughter. Give her all of her space with miraculous force of love let go of the burdens of waiting, accept daughter comes to teach her father on his path of life."

And here the roles inverse, accompanying the hand becomes mediator to express inner wisdom.

Muriel's text is a living example:

"Liberty is living each instant without fear of the following instant; Liberty is not a word that lives in me, however, in my heart, well hidden, I am freer than those who answer the expectations for the glory of the world. For me, there is no beginning, no end. The instant waits for the following instant, in the infinite unfolding of time going by. I am suspended between two instants, suspended on the lips of time. I dream of dancing the circle of time and sing to be reborn the next instant."

This liberty is compromised by the troubles that affect Muriel. Accompanied Inner Communication creates an opening in the prison of her body:

"Words warm me, comfort me and calm me. They are my liberator."

Florence expresses it in this way: *"I weave with you a cloth of words that reconnects me with a hidden part of me. Like a squirrel regaining liberty outside of his cage."*

When talking about the atmosphere in the establishment where she lives and her visions of the situation, Geneviève writes:

"The Christ lives in everyone's heart, it is easier for those who know and accept. I see this spark more and more clearly in each person."

I have found this transcendent dimension of conscience in each person unable to speak whom I have accompanied. The way they express it varies in function of the family context. Anne-Christine, who was brought up in a Protestant family, wrote with my support:

"The Christ is in our hearts to unite the worlds. Christ lives in the heart, the heart holds the key. To put oneself in heart that contains presence of Christ is so simple."

Muriel's family does not adhere to any religious practice. She wrote:

"I see several chapters separated by a wall of life."

I questioned *"What is a wall of life?"*

She answered: *"The wall of life is when we go from one level to another to contact another life memory. I am teaching you metaphysics. I help you understand the functioning of the worlds that are in the world. I survive thanks to my vision of the worlds gathered together in the heart of God."*

I still do not understand what Muriel is trying to say. As I explain this to her, she answers:

"Don't try to understand. I am talking about the life inside. The world we cannot see with eyes and knows the back of the eye through transparency. The negative of the photo of life. Headache to try and find designation to name the unnamable because I feel I can say it differently. Find line of time, walk between the words and choose those that show up on the ribbon."

This young woman who suffers from autistic disorders shows how I am the one who is disabled, on certain levels:

"You are still caterpillar, stuck in your rut, closed within circles of matter. I see differently. I look from above, like the butterfly that left his chrysalis and flies away, way up high in the sky. The butterfly flies away and leaves his shell below, deposited on a blade of grass."

This inner life which is beyond the person is a source of suffering which is difficult to express. With the help of AIC and by accompanying the gesture, a space where words can be deposited is formed:

"I plagiarize words to enliven what is inside. So then I can come out of my cocoon."

Anne-Christine is a 57 year old adult suffering from autistic disorders and does not speak at all. She describes what she feels and connects her with each person and the "Whole"[13]:

"Limit of you and me is deep, yet I cannot find the limit and I do not limit my own outline. Mutism comes from indefinite limits. The proximity of words limits my speech. The words are there and I cannot say them. I am in the unity of All That Is, I feel, I know and limit within me fades."

Anne-Christine needs to touch all of the objects that are in her environment. She describes it like this:

"Freedom to touch to appropriate world. I perceive all, all, all, and it is stronger than me, I cannot do otherwise (...) I sort the visible and invisible. I see the invisible and touching gives me the texture of what is visible. Mutism makes the world in its globality present in my head and differentiation is difficult."

Accompanied Inner Communication helps her: *"Holes of silence widen to clearings of words."*

Muriel evokes her access to the transpersonal field:

"Deep down, I exult to be the one who knows what is happening behind threads of destiny. Juxtaposition of words to tell my difference. I know

the things beyond time and I trace a line to separate yesterday from today. Do you know I live outside of time? I am a sponge that adopts within its bumps and dents all of the detours connected between themselves by the thread of destiny. Go between the lines and see the cross-country skiers' tracks become clear in the snow."

There is an immense contradiction between the depths of what is felt, the thoughts expressed with the accompanied gesture and the behavior of most people who cannot speak. Physical or mental challenges often prevent people from leaving their mark in social life. Thanks to accompanying the gesture of the hand, written work is born which gives them a place in the social community.

In my viewpoint, the process itself of Accompanied Inner Communication seems to be a marvelous testimony of unity in that the facilitator and the facilitated person become one, during the session. This is in resonance with the feeling of unity lived within, beyond the veil of what is visible. We could say that these texts are a co-creation because the facilitator lends his cognitive system, his brain acts as a data base available for use by the person expressing himself/herself. In the book written by Gilbert Pierre and his daughter Anne-Christine[17], texts typed with four different facilitators are quoted. It is interesting to note that in all cases, the themes addressed by Anne-Christine are recurring and almost identical, even if the form varies in function of the facilitator.

The accompaniment with Accompanied Inner Communication of people who cannot speak, or who cannot speak very much, does not reduce the disability. During the AIC sessions, it opens a space of communication and better well-being. For the person writing, it also gives him back his emotional experiences, which helps contribute to restoring the conscience of his own being and liberating him from what has become a heavy weight.

The texts also give precious information about emotional experiences thus helping close relations to modify their actions in the best way. Close relations are not always conscience of what is going on inside and they work at protecting the non-speaking person by pushing away emotions that come up, however it would be more judicious to put these feelings into words because they are perceived – no matter what. Understanding the receptive capacity of people with disabilities will help spark an authentic exchange.

AIC shows that behind the suffering personality, the Self is still intact; no matter what the disability is. The depth of the underlying comprehension of the typed text creates questions. Most people suffering from a disability help us go forward, make us look at life from a different angle. They are the *"children that deceive their appearances"* to show us that *"The essential is invisible for the eyes"* and bring to earth *"their love potion"*.

Through what they type, their wounds participate in our self-realization and invite us to look at our own wounds as a springboard towards the realization of our potentials.

The next chapter is dedicated to examining this theme in more depth.

Chapter 6

Transcend the wounds of the past to create a catalyst for self fulfillment

Snippets of the past emerge in Accompanied Inner Communication so that what was pushed aside can be reintegrated in the psyche. Most of the time it is a traumatic incident that the memory has buried to preserve the person from unmanageable pain. This work of releasing repressed memories into consciousness is done progressively and always spontaneously, in function of what the conscience can handle. The goal is not at all to go hunting in one's past nor out of curiosity; that would be contrary to the ethics of our technique.

A PATH TO SELF

The objective is to let emerge what the person needs, so as to live his present with increased consciousness. So, the appearance of the past becomes a catalyzing element helping us on our evolutionary path.

Experience has shown me how much each difficulty traversed is in effect a beacon indicating the path of self-fulfillment. The potential force that exists in each of us is often on the other side of the encountered suffering. In this way, each obstacle carries within it the seed of its own solution which becomes an asset – once it has been overcome.

Patrick's case is meaningful:

The meaning given to the difficulties he has encountered is explained in this text:

"I chose this difficult path to heal a past life and to root myself within compassion which transcends anger and hate. Temporary loss of sight helped transcendence."

In this case there is a link with what was lived during gestation: *"Barren swimming closes my view. Right to live is threatened. Blindness of cheerful lad is solution to survive."* And an old memory: *"Violence of jubilant people affected me in my integrity. Blindness programmed so as not to see unbearable unleashing of violence."*

Patrick, who carried a memory affecting his integrity, relived this event inside his mother. The mother's desire to welcome a child was affected by her incapacity to truly welcome him.

A PATH TO SELF

Even though he says he needs to *"transcend anger and hate"* he incarnates in exactly this context which immediately confronts him with a form of violence. He survives, but has weak eyesight. His body reconnects with an old program. Highlighting this program allows him to understand what he came to resolve and liberated him of an old pattern. In a way, his suffering takes on meaning; he can release the painful memories and move on to something else.

With the concurrent help of an orthoptist, Christian's eyesight improved progressively.

Personally, important changes took place. His experiences have led him to align himself today with his essential spiritual goal. After retiring, he has been moving towards what Bernard Montaud refers to as « the Task", that means "My type of service on Earth, (...) where no one else can do what I need to do»[1814].

When we look at something it has effects. Quantum physics has shown us that the observer has an effect on the object observed. This is true for everything. So looking at someone else with his force and his capacity to traverse what life gives him, reinforces him. Accompanied Inner Communication helps the person connect with his own power.

To welcome ones force is to dare express it. We have often denied aspects of our self to conform to what our relations expect of us. We have adopted a low profile so that we do not disturb, or we have reduced our fantasy to correspond to a social norm. In this way Capucine's creativity is limited by her fears of being judged.

Her propensity for self criticism makes her prisoner of an image of herself that does not correspond. She is very self-demanding and very sensitive to how others judge her. She needs to liberate herself from her fear of judgment to freely express her own truth. She has progressed a lot, however vulnerability to criticism still blocks the creative process.

Capucine is a novelist and loves to feel rocked by the words that emerge with fluidity. The farther she advances in her book, the more fluidly the words flow. Great joy accompanies this creative process. She showed the beginning of her book to someone she fully trusted. (Was there an error in discernment?) That person vigorously criticized the chosen theme and called the pages "insipid". The shock was violent and for several years Capucine was not able to write.

She came to see me, and this is what she typed in Accompanied Inner Communication:

"Miniscule, see well that I feel like a very young wounded girl. I cannot react, nor take my place in front of those I esteem. I say self esteem is like a destabilized balance. I push with all my weight on the lower tray and cannot climb up the slope. Tears bump into each other inside me mixed with quiet unspeakable rage. It is as if I am unable to speak, gagged with words empty of life. I say that everything gets mixed up, quickly unweave cloth of doubts, un-mix. Criticism vibrates disharmonious

chord of esteem of myself. In me, the child goes to background for shame of being seen as feeble. Look at mocking from another time to rehabilitate the child. I can barely speak and mix my words, mocked by my brothers and father who abandon me and laugh at me.

My words are beautiful and I am proud. I make them slowly as I understand. Tragedy to be mocked in innocent creation because humiliation is lived by child. Solitude and abandon, father is my constant ally and here it is that he joins the clan of mocking brothers. Kindness to reinstate the child."

The criticism by her colleague awoke a childhood wound, and so, the adult overtaken by the wounded child, could not find the resources necessary for the correct positioning. This young woman felt devastated by the criticism and could not answer appropriately, thus giving reason to her worst enemy.

Nevertheless this painful episode will be positive because it will allow Capucine to reconnect with the happiness she felt before.

From her youth, Capucine loved words; she associated them with her fantasy, and made new ones to express what she felt deep inside as precisely as possible. Little by little she denied her creative fantasy to blend in and avoid being mocked.

Feeling the humiliation of the child mocked by her brothers allowed her to take the young girl in her heart and to thank her for the entire road travelled.

A PATH TO SELF

The criticism of her friend reconnected her with a powerful creative force. The qualifier: insipid, reflects her need of approval which limited her creative fervor and reduced the expression of her element of fantasy. This criticism is actually a positive current showing her what she is capable of.

As to the teasing by her brothers, maybe they were a bit jealous of this inventive young sister. The admiration she had for her elders incited the child to submit to a structured rigor so that she was congratulated rather than teased. Capucine's creativity will finally be transformed to reflect her true nature. In AIC she writes:

"Infinite joy to reconnect with who I am. Quit all protocols and no limits for creativity to reveal my true identity. I am daughter of wind and dunes, words carry me like a thoroughbred on the desert sand and I gallop to express the wind's song on the strand. Arid structure disciplined my natural vagabond. Integrated are the rules of language, I can defy them joyously to go beyond the limits and sing the words of the heart on the on the course of the current that carries me. Thank you."

So as you can see, on the flip side of the difficulties encountered there is a strong creative inventiveness. Regarding people with a disability, the roles seem inversed.

Accompanied Inner Communication promotes listening to the person and restores speech to the author to help him live with the totality of his Self. Often, disabilities go together with an incarnation difficulty that we need to hear so that the body, spirit and heart can work together in the person's life, in a time and space that the person can fully appropriate for himself. AIC is a communication tool, opening a space for expression. In this space, the largest difficulties become witnesses to wisdom and an unsuspected conscience.

By accompanying the person with a handicap to write via AIC, it is easier for them to find their place in this world and to give us messages destined to help us grow. In this way, our "jobs" are reversed and the exchange between the person giving and the person receiving is respected while the dignity of each person is honored. Annick also insists on the notion of difference. Here is the text that this non -speaking adult gives us, helped by her mother who facilitated her communication:

"We are not that different, different from you. We do not talk, we are deprived of words, and you, and it is so hard for you to say things, to say what is bothering you, to tell your truth. You go around in circles; the mimics of your body betray your words. You are traitors to yourself. For us, even if you have problems understanding us, we are always sincere, congruent; our heart is always in phase with our attitude.

Learn to understand us, open the ears of your heart and you will hear our messages. Sounds that don't make sounds, chords without notes.

We have so much to tell you, so much to teach you. Do not abuse our patience. Now you know, and I am the witness, if you listen to us, we have so much to tell you, to show you that the disability that you see is not a difference of humanity, it is just an appearance.

Humanity is located in the heart of each person. We are the humanity of tomorrow. That which awakens compassion in you, not pity. That which allows you to go past your boundaries, go past your limits to understand that the invisible things are much more important than you can imagine.

We are the creators of the new world where the capacity to Love is much more important than the ambition to have, a new world where everyone will have the right to a spot in the sun, fully in the Light.

I invite you into this new world, I take your hand and I lead you, let go of your fears, let go of your brakes, and so nothing holds you back any longer. It is so easy to have confidence, believe me, that is what I do every day.

Me, Annick, Daughter of Joy"

This text by Annick is a big YES to her life, as it is. This yes is the essential step on ones path to oneselfs. In the book Hara, K.G.Dürckheim expresses it like this: *"The path is an unconditional yes to what is".*

This acceptation includes the acceptation of the family we are born into. And that yes, is not always the easiest to say. Accompanied Inner Communication can help us find the meaning of our incarnation in the family we were born into.

Chapter 7

Say yes to Life as it presents itself to access the resources of our family tree

- **Say yes to our family tree**

Our family tree can be thought of as a base that holds us. Our ascendants are like our roots. Acknowledging them and giving them their place in our heart participates in our being well grounded. It is also by saying yes to our origins that we can have access to the resources of our family tree. It is interesting to note that the disciplines that require solid grounding, like aikido and tai chi, come from countries where they worship ancestors.

A PATH TO SELF

Certainly we carry in our memories the pain of our ancestors as well as the programs they developed as a response to their living conditions and the traumatic shocks they encountered. We also carry within ourselves numerous resources we have inherited from our ascendants. Our psyche is rich with the past; our ancestors left us gifts that are part of our artistic and spiritual inheritance. It might be a special predisposition that contributes to excelling in a subject, music, painting or gifts as a therapist.

To begin with, the texts that come out in Accompanied Inner Communication allow the transformation of memories.

For several months I accompanied Christine, who had an auto-immune illness that blocked her tears. It seems that there were several factors that contributed to the emergence of this illness. A feeling of guilt transmitted by her grandmother and present in her cellular memory and reactivated at her birth. With me Christine typed:

"Ancestor left with a child to take care of, death the traitor cut bond of responsibility. My painful birth reactivated memory of blame. I thought I would kill mother when forcing passage to life. Joy to transcend field of blame for pardon of self."

Afterwards, she confirmed that her grandmother died very young leaving behind several young children.

During a later session Christine wrote:

A PATH TO SELF

"Memory of grandmother follows me, drowning alive is recuperated in my cellular memory. (…) I transgress the law of inheritance, curse is cancelled."

Today Christine once again has tears. A homeopathic doctor treated her for several years while she undertook other initiatives to understand the meaning of her illness. I think that these various therapies facilitated a transformation on many levels to include recovery. Medical treatment was a central element and Accompanied Inner Communication was without a doubt a liberating trigger.

Marie, of Chilean origin, suffered from an illness forcing her to be immobile. During a session, she evoked an event that she was later able to validate with her paternal grandmother:

"Fear of death in tree (the family tree). It is death of grandmother in tragic life. Fear, fraud, horrible noise, archaic fear of being buried alive."

Marie's great grandmother had in effect almost been buried alive in an earthquake. This old memory was still present. The session facilitated a liberation which symbolically re-connected her with the family tree. *"Joy to dig under root of pain, energy circulates freely, tree of lives becomes green."*

Expressions like ; trees of life become green or tree turns green again appear relatively often at the end of texts typed with me, in connection with the previous expression of a transgenerational life.

It seems that symbolically the traces of an ancestor's traumatic life experiences stop the sap from circulating freely in the family tree. Expression of the suffering connected to that life experience releases the blockage and allows the energy of life to reach all of the branches of the tree.

AIC also allows us to become conscious of what cuts or separates us from our resources. Recognizing the connection that unites us as ascendants, starting with our parents, allows us to draw freely from the resources that our genealogical tree possesses.

- **Say yes to our Fathers and Mothers**

Alexandra came to see me to understand the reason for her lack of confidence and to try and remedy that.

Alexandra's mother is French and her father is English. Her father remained true to his country and loyal to his family. He often goes back to Great Britain to see his brothers and sisters. He left his country to rejoin the woman he loved. He speaks English at home and has never really spoken French well.

Alexandra feels as though she has no roots, she doesn't feel connected to any culture. She speaks English fluently but is not drawn to England and has not gone back for several years.

She studied science for many years and has a steady job, but one that does not bring her joy. She would like to spend all her time painting yet explains that her father would be very worried if she followed her objective. Her current job corresponds to what her father expects. She does not feel she has the courage to disappoint him. Alexandra has an older sister and it seems that her father had really wanted a boy at her birth. In Accompanied Inner Communication, she expresses this in the following way:

"Fear to do wrongly is transmitted by father and affected me as soon as I emerged into this world. Am I the one he is expecting? I feel caught in the middle and I need father's approval. Disrepute put on me as baby I feel insufficient (as) little girl. Being woman necessitates separating from desire my father had to father a son.

I know father's love very present; it is just old memory of tiny baby."

Up to now, Alexandra had made most of her choices in function of her father's expectations. However, she had grown distant with the family origins and so at that level, she lacked loyalty. During an AIC session, she clearly expresses her need to show loyalty to her father: *"Liberty is stated with total acknowledgement of paternal ancestors."*

To begin with, Alexandra became conscious that because of her rejection of England she was cut from her roots and was in an awkward position with her father. First she had to fully accept her English origins to find her roots and remain loyal to her paternal origins. Then she could progressively begin professional changes and explain to her father how she wished to orient herself towards a different life choice.

The acceptation of her British origins would also allow her to reconnect with all of the resources of those descendents. At the same time, as long as she rejects the paternal origins, guilt feelings force her to compensate this rejection by being true to the image her father projects on her.

She studied science and chose a career that satisfied her father's hopes, thus betraying her own desires.

By accepting her father without any restrictions, Alexandra can fully tap into the integrality of the life she received. It is precisely this total acceptation that gives her the liberty to live her life as she desires; without the fear of not living up to her father's expectations.

Loyalty gives us wings, welcoming what is, frees us. By entering straight into the life that is given to us, we can seize the opportunities for growth that are proposed to us.

Each of us is confronted with specific difficulties that seem like fragility to begin with, yet become a force, once the trial linked to this related weakness is transcended.

It seems that each of us comes into the world in a unique context favoring the blooming of certain qualities, putting us in front of specific reoccurring difficulties, inviting us to go beyond the situations that could imprison us otherwise.

The fact of being born into such and such a family or not, does not matter if we consider that the events we encounter are an opportunity to help love grow within us. I see life as a path for growth, an invitation to love always more and better.

This is just a hypothesis: Maybe our Soul, conscious of its weaknesses and strengths, chooses the family that it wants to incarnate into in function of the possibilities of growth that it would be given? Seen in this light, family traumatisms become a launch pad for our evolution. Thus, the difficult situations will repeat themselves until we have understood what we have to transcend.

I clearly experienced this myself when I confronted the feeling of being repeatedly forgotten, or abandoned. In my family, abandonment repeated itself: my grandmother was raised in an orphanage, my grandfather died on the battlefield in 1917, leaving a wife alone with two young children - one of whom was my father, four years old. My father in turn was then abandoned by his mother who entrusted him for a while to her parents-in-law in Paris.

Being the only child of a mother with heart problems for whom procreation was strictly forbidden, I, in my way, learned that my presence could tire my mother. So, from the age of four, I spent all my vacations including three months each summer, in a home for children, which became my second family. My mother died when I was fifteen years old. My father's second marriage with a very young woman incited me to put a distance between us and fend for myself at a young age. ....leave, yet feel abandoned at the same time.....I married a very considerate and generous man, however the feeling of abandon repeated itself in that his profession forced him to travel abroad very frequently. As a young woman, it was very hard for me to accept these trips until I finally understood. Curiously, as soon as I could calmly accept my temporary solitude, my husband's trips became less frequent. As if once the lesson was learned, life stopped giving us the difficulty.

With one of my Accompanied Inner Communication colleagues, I typed:
"Understand well that in this life abandon was my lifeline. I want to say that the path of the burning wound was the road to conscience of mu unified Self."

The path of the wound can become the road to conscience. Because we have marked the path that takes us away from pain, we become experts in the art of manifesting the symmetric potential of the original wound. For example, being abandoned can generate the aptitude to abandon oneself, to adapt easily to life's unexpected events.

Life also carries within it the solutions to its own contradictions: After my high school diploma I finally decided to study German, whereas I was drawn more to medicine and psychology. I never really understood what motivated my choice. From the age of eighteen, I had the burning desire to adopt a child….without knowing why I had this wish. Today, I understand now that I was pushed by an unconscious desire to make up for the times my ascendants were abandoned. I was totally surprised when I worked on my family tree and noticed that my grandfather – who died at war-, had exactly the same birthday as our adopted daughter.

My unconscious choices were definitely enlightened with therapeutic work. In a state of modified conscience, I saw a flash of my father when he was very young, holding hands with a very small boy. The official family history made me the oldest of four children born from three different marriages. My father was 38 years old when I was born. He lived in Berlin for a while and was probably there in 1933 because he told me a story about the burning of the Reichstag. I know very little about his life at that time, I only have the memory that he spoke German perfectly. My grandmother was Alsatian (from western France in Alsace) and worked from 1921 to 1922 in Wiesbaden, Germany as a secretary in an office dealing with the French occupation. My father, who was a handsome young man of 21, possibly had an affair with a German woman during his time in Germany. Was a child born from that union? Times were difficult and my father had to leave Germany quickly to rejoin the army. He was drafted in Toulouse, France at the end of 1933.

I will never know if the flash I had in therapy corresponds to a reality. I have no way of validating the fact that I may have a half brother in Germany, seventeen years older than me. However, with my subconscious pushing me to study German, it created a connection with my father's possible partner and the adoption becomes reparation for my father abandoning his German child.

I have always thought that the objective in our incarnation was to learn to always love more. When we accept this consciously, the circumstances surrounding this incarnation can become a gift of life pushing us towards more and more love.

♥ Say yes to one's conception and birth

As we have already seen, the texts typed in Accompanied Inner Communication help us understand the meanings of difficulties encountered. Sometimes the difficulty is harsh, and it necessitates a long period of maturation to be able to accept what happened. Often, the difficulties begin at birth and even in the womb.

In my book "Les voix de la main" [915] (The voices of the hand) I describe Paul's situation – he was born even though his mother had an intrauterine contraceptive device. All his life Paul felt he was at the wrong place at the wrong time, and that he always turned up at the worst possible moment. He was born prematurely when his family was on vacation. His arrival upset everyone. He writes in AIC:

"Dead end, blocked in the funnel life is strangled. It is like coming into the world without being invited. It's an old refrain and my being is tired of this same old story. Belief that life takes me by surprise and hinders display of great force. My power is cut, strangled. Go look at my conception. I defy rules and implant life where non-life is programmed. Conception is like refrain cutting me in two. Life than wins loses, life that loses wins. Let go, let go of all control and welcome to be loser to win the bet. Because I thought I was condemned to a non-life I defied death for victory of life. Great force accompanies my steps. See clearly that turnaround of my conscience is unavoidable step. I say, I thought I was the unexpected one and I quickly made that my rule of life. I arrive unexpectedly and lock access to path of recognition by fear of not being received."

In his profession, Paul is a pioneer. But his innovative ideas are not always well received. The first part of his life was devoted to defying what was known, as if it was a precocious preparation for the place that would become his in society.

"Priority is to love the child I was and the adult I am. So defying is without arrogance. Contact force and see that hindrance is in truth an aspect of my specificity. I am he who defies the rules to open up a new way of looking. Hindrance becomes catalyst and springboard as soon as I accept who I am beyond what appears. Dare to open new area to set up my cooperation in connection with value of heart. Return to see tiny baby who believes he his bothersome, to glorify his tenacity, because I

became winner of life I was, and winner I am once again. Expanding viewpoint opens overall vision. Innovate in welcoming current step is my path. Joy, liberation reached each one of my cells. Thank you."

Paul is the person who jumps over fences and goes forward. His fears of being a hindrance made him accept behavior that was a disservice. By accepting to play the role he had chosen; that of pioneer, he could leave the fear of being a hindrance. Thus, the discomfort that emanates from him sometimes, transforms itself into persuasive force. Only he can give himself the recognition he needs. So, he becomes convincing. His strongest difficulty becomes his strength as soon as he accepts his specificity as innovator.

The task is even more difficult when the conception is followed by a true rejection with an attempt to abort. However, the triumph of the force of Life is testimony to a force and a desire to live that is very powerful. The wound will be like a rejection. This is what happened to Josiane, who I evoked in a previous book [16] ; Josiane found herself constantly confronted with a situation of rejection. Regarding the time in her mother's womb, with AIC she typed:

"Desire of non-life for me puts me in danger. I make myself small, very small, I curl up, life continues but I keep immense fear of being rejected. Words are balm on my painful heart. Love and Light surround the tiny baby who is me, like a well meaning cloud. I slowly dare take my place."

A PATH TO SELF

Josiane confirmed that when she was conceived as the fifth child in the family, her mother was overwhelmed by the care and attention she had to give her four young children. Rejection is Josiane's original wound. Her fear of rejection is so powerful that she manages her distress by anticipating the situations of rejection, thus provoking them. With AIC she writes:

"Finally accept myself to be accepted. For many lives I have denigrated myself, disowned myself. The exterior reflects the image I have of myself. Rejection of who I am puts me in awkward position with life. I pass contradictory messages and am victim of my own machinations. I hold onto rejection not to lose my identity. Yet my soul hopes to emerge from this dilemma."

All of her therapeutic work consisted in accepting herself with her history, without subtracting anything. Little by little, once the wound had transformed,

Josiane became confident and now expresses her creativity by painting and drawing. The transformed original wound became the propellant to facilitate her artistic expression. With Accompanied Inner Communication she expressed:

"Deep down inside me a calm and silent child radiant and full of hidden potentials waits to be seen and recognized. My memories of childhood drawings that delighted my entourage, take the paintbrush to express my inner

wealth, finally dare to be me, dare to loosen the lines of the portrait I keep in my heart. I am landscape architect of souls; I know how to dive into hearts to read the vast perspectives of iridescent colors."

Josiane took painting lessons and developed her creative potential. By accepting herself she progressively became well known. I heard from her recently and she told me that her exhibitions were more and more successful.

Saying yes to life as it presents itself at birth is certainly an enormous task in some cases.

Let's take Valerie's case. She came to see me to quit a resistance to life that incited her to systematically refuse everything that was suggested. Her couple was in danger. Her work was slowed down by her negative reaction to each new proposition that her boss made. Valerie knew she must change her behavior but her resistance was like a force that controlled her willpower. She was also fed up that her husband made all of her decisions for her. She was ashamed of her negative reactions to the vacations suggested by her thoughtful companion, but here again; she couldn't control her inopportune anger.

From the first session, her birth was evoked in the text she typed with my accompaniment:

"Say life is like taken hostage with no desire to go forward. I am nice and warm in uterus, not yet

ready for the big moment. Sudden contraction tightening, I feel propelled without understanding, life contracts, never ending tunnel and I am like a toy in the body of life, transported, pushed unbeknownst to me outside of stomach. Terror, it is like decision was made without my agreement and I brake without being able to control the advancement. Terror, it is too early, don't want to, not yet. Joy to put words. Finally liberation is possible; I did not have time to desire to be born and this no to my birth happens again and again with each new situation. Joy to finally understand and unwind the thread to reclaim my birth. Reclaim my birth to finally say yes, say yes to my beginning of life, say yes, a big yes to life. Relief, thank you, thank you, thank you."

Valerie knows that the doctor had decided to induce her birth because it was ten days past term. The decision was taken as a precaution, fear was the driving force and there was no room to take into consideration the experience of the baby to be born. Her desire to be born is short circuited. Becoming conscious of this old memory liberated Valerie and allowed her to become the subject of her decisions without necessarily rejecting suggestions.

In this example, we can see how not having the time to access the desire to be born provokes difficulties to agree to the desires of others. Valerie realized that it is as if her birth had been stolen from her. From her helplessness as a newborn, anger was reactivated each time someone made a decision for her.

A PATH TO SELF

Bringing these memories to light allowed Valerie to finally agree to her life and part with the resistances to suggestions made by others.

In all of these testimonies, it is a conscious Yes to what life presents that permits resistances to progressively decrease leaving room for acceptation which opens the doors to the resources and realization of potentials.

Once the words have described a past action, there is a liberating effect almost instantaneously. The liberation remains if the person consciously decides to take responsibility for his/her life and the thoughts he/she maintains.

However, as I have already remarked, the situation is different and almost turned around when talking about accompanying people with disabilities: often the family members have a hard time fully accepting this painful situation which puts an end to the idolized image a parent has of his child. This text which was typed by Lucie in AIC and facilitated by her mother bears witness to the mystery that surrounds the situations of handicap and the distance to be covered by family and friends to say yes to this situation:

« Let me choose to become a child at God's service. The path is not via normality; all the people who wish me to be normal violently compel me to stay stuck in an infernal "interspace".

A PATH TO SELF

For me, becoming who I am supposed to become, is accepting that my evolutionary path is on a different road.

The path of my evolution is attached to yours and certain people.

My reason for being is simple and if you accept to accompany me – completely – without any hope that one day you will see me, Lucile Vialard, a young girl who talks, walks and goes to school, well then I will be able to show you other things.

Let me become what I am supposed to become; my reason for existing is not in this body. It is my atrophied body that serves to liberate me and connects me so easily to another reality. In that reality, I am the most normal of the most normal and no one would think of changing me." [17]

If the handicap follows an accident, everyone's life will be completely turned upside down. In this case, the Yes will be a long road, going through a long tunnel which can always open out to unexpected horizons thanks to a complete inner turnaround.

My work has helped me become conscious that the people unable to speak are very often closer to the values of Being than people without disabilities: Behind the suffering body, the soul expresses itself. When physical disorders prevent a person from developing the values of having, and deprive them of the advantages and pleasures connected to the world of appearances, a strong, demanding inner power develops.

A PATH TO SELF

It is these same people who gave us Accompanied Communication of the heart, as it pleases me to call this technique. Thanks to this method of communication we create a space of expression for them.

Life draws us towards a vaster conscience. What seems to be a truth one day can be questioned the next day with new awareness. In this way a multitude of truths coexist, each one corresponding to a reality.

People with a disability that deprives them from the possibility of speaking, have access to a "vastness" that often exceeds us. So they are the ones, who thanks to the accompaniment, participate in changing our references, push us to go higher and make us grow. Thanks to them and AIC, they help us to challenge our viewpoints and outlook on "traditional" live.

In any case there is a very strong connection, and through this connection, every person is in the words of Jean Vannier [18]"a sacred story".

Conclusion

There is a marvelous potential for love in each of us that manifests itself when space opens that is favorable for its expression.

Rapidly, my accompanying work showed me how closely we are all connected and responsible we are for the world we are living in. Lastly, my inner universe determines the outer universe I live in. It is like the materialization of my inner universe and the conflicts that I live in my outer universe are the barometer of my inner conflicts.

Becoming conscious of the responsibility we have in our life allows us to leave the state of victim and to take charge of our future with dignity. We are mutually supportive and I affect those who are close to me whenever I allow my aggressiveness free rein.

The work by the Japanese researcher Masaru Emoto is living proof of the impact of our thoughts and our words, on the world around us. Mr. Emoto took microscopic photos of water crystals in test tubes that he had previously spoken different words to or had labeled. He showed that the frozen water crystals had been transformed when specific and converging thoughts were directed at them.

This is what he says about his work: " The water exposed to the word "thank you" presents marvelous crystals with a well-formed hexagonal shape, whereas the water where the word "idiot" had been attached to the test tube, presented deformed and fractioned crystals". [1]

Given that man is made up of 75% water, I can deduce that if I surround my life with a space of love and gratitude I transform myself and I then have a positive effect on those I meet.

Becoming aware of this contributes to one of the objectives underlying my work. The fact of being put in contact with a force of love in one's psyche helps the person I am accompanying to put more and more conscience in his everyday life. It will also help him release the self judgment he submits himself to and also those who cross his path.

Accompaniment is an essential element in the technique I teach. One of the goals of this accompaniment is to help the person consulting to stop judging himself, to accept himself as he is and

---

[1] Masaru Emoto, « *Messages from Water*»

also to accept what life presents with as little resistance as possible. AIC does not pretend to have a new theory about man or his life. However, it cannot be considered as a simple technique or treatment. Accompanied Inner Communication allows each accompanied person to better structure himself and live his own life, free from unconscious loyalties and useless attachments.

A text written in Accompanied Inner Communication expresses a feeling. It has no value as historical truth, testimony or evidence. The texts are the expression of the present moment and are unique to the session.

AIC is a posture, a welcome, an accompaniment.

Listening is an essential aspect of Accompanied Inner Communication. The person connects to his inner self with the help of the AIC texts and the sensitive listening.

If this technique elicits questions, it also gives immense hope which participates in each person's meaning of life.

A PATH TO SELF

Here is a special note for this book by the translator's « disabled » daughter:

"Souls in pain need voices to speak. Unbearable imprisonment in straightjacket of silence.
All of the people unable to speak are crying out with all their being, deprived of freely expressing themselves.
Weight of silence provokes explosive repressions; it is urgently needed to hear the call of all these people not able to speak – no matter what their life story may be.
I know that this call for help has already been heard, thank you."
Jenny

A mother's note:

"My disabled daughter was my guide on the path to Inner Communication. She helped me – as did her brother and sister – realize that it is possible to communicate with the inner part of your child (or any other person).
I became very conscious of the possibility of written inner communication when I started training with Martine in Accompanied Inner Communication (in French and in France). I remember Jenny's first written communication, it was like letting the water free from behind a dam. She was so grateful and happy that I had "discovered" this method and that I was able to acknowledge and communicate with

her inner self. It was a true liberation of her inner self!

It is so easy to think of people who seem different as being really different, but down deep, they are just like us; it is only the outside that differs. Even though I can communicate on the level of Inner Self, Jenny still is disabled and many things are still difficult in her daily life. The difference is that I am aware of two levels of communication: the inner non-verbal level and the common speech mode.

What does this mean? That when I speak to my disabled daughter with speech, I need to dialogue at her conscious intellectual and emotional level.

However, I can communicate and inform her inner self on a different level, and that helps her conscious aspect to better accept less joyous everyday situations (like leaving home to go back to her adult living center).

It is like working on two layers. The first layer is able to accept everything and be incredibly spiritual and one with Spirit and the second layer has a mental age of four.

To conclude, even though it is often difficult to take care of a dependent person, my acceptation of her disabilities has completely changed now that I can consciously communicate with Jenny on these two levels. I appreciate her presence and thank her for her love and for being with us and helping us learn so much. Her joy of life and acceptance of others is a lesson for all!"

A PATH TO SELF

The deontology for the practice of Accompanied Inner Communication

<u>Training:</u>

The training of Accompanied Inner Communication is primarily for health care professionals. However, it is possible to accept people who have completed personal therapeutic work and who are concurrently training in the field of heath care.

The accompaniment with Inner Communication is demanding and requires constant work on oneself to avoid or reduce as much as possible, the projections and transfers that are inherent to our human quality.

It is composed of 6 modules that are obligatory for everyone.

Between two modules, it is requested that the trainees practice, if possible between themselves and also participate in the revision-practice sessions.

Personal therapeutic work is also required parallel to the training. It is the guarantor of professional integrity and helps avoid confusion with one's personal history.

<u>Practically:</u>

- Accompanied Inner Communication is done by holding the hand of the person who has come to be accompanied, thus in his presence. It is a

practice that implies accompanying the gesture of the accompanied person above a computer keyboard to allow the expression of an experience that is inexprimable with conscious speech.
- Accompanying people with disabilities sometimes requires the practitioner to adapt his accompaniment to the motor or neuromuscular difficulties of the person typing.

Accompanying non-disabled people:

- The accompaniment with AIC is done with the intention to allow the accompanied person to live the present with increased conscience and feelings of harmony. Any attitude of curiosity is incompatible with this practice.
- The practitioner does not interpret what has been expressed via the keyboard. He refers the accompanied person to his feelings, in relation to what he typed. However, if needed, he will decode the metaphors that emerge.
- The practitioner is respectful of the beliefs of each person and in no way tries to influence him.
- Confidentiality: The contents of the texts are strictly confidential.
- When accompanying children, this confidentiality must be respected. If it seems desirable to share certain aspects of the text with the parent present, the child must be asked for permission.
- The accompanier does not intervene in any possible aspect of medical prescriptions, or in police investigations.

A PATH TO SELF

Accompanying non-speaking people

- In the sense that AIC is also an alternative method of communication, the session can be interactive and the parent accompanying the person would in this case, be present in the room during the session.
- However, in all cases a confidential space will be foreseen during the session itself.
- In an institution or in connection with an institution: the typed texts are confidential and should in no way become part of the institution's files.
- It is up to the person typing in AIC with the support of the accompanier, to decide whether or not the texts should be shared.

The typed texts:

- In all cases, a text typed in Accompanied Inner Communication expresses a feeling. It has no value as a truthful historical event or as testimony.
- The texts are exclusively the expression of a unique present moment, that of the session.

A PATH TO SELF

Notes

---

[1] The word "Shaman" (chaman in French) officially entered the French language in 1842 and comes from the word "saman" of the Toungouses tribe means "person who posses Knowledge". It is the word chosen by the first Russian anthropologists to designate individuals who practiced specific spiritual practices and fulfilled characteristic functions in their communities.

[2]: Books written by Pierre Weil The Silent Revolution (autobiography).
The Art of Living in Peace, UNESCO, 2000.

[3] Michael Roads, Through the Eyes of Love, book 1, 2, 3, Six Degrees Publishing Group inc.

[4] John Eccles, How the conscience controls the brain

[5] Constanze Lang is an author specializing in the theme of Family and Systemic Constellations. A founding member and Vice President of the International Systemic Constellation Association (ISCA) 2007-2011. She practices and has taught Systemic Constellations since 1993. Also in charge of part of the training program for a post-graduate degree in   family

clinical and systemic practices at the Paris University VIII. Participates in training prgrams abroad, for example in Sweden, Russia, Singapore, China and Germany.

[6] Bert Hellinger (born 16 December 1925, in Leimen, Baden, Germany as Anton Hellinger) is a German psychotherapist associated with a therapeutic method best known as Family Constellations and Systemic Constellations

[7] Virginia Satir is one of the key figures in the development of family therapy. She believed that a healthy family life involved an open and reciprocal sharing of affection, feelings, and love. Satir made enormous contributions to family therapy in her clinical practice and training. She began treating families in 1951 and established a training program for psychiatric residents at the Illinois State Psychiatric Institute in 1955.

[8] Dr. Jacob (Jakob) Levy Moreno (18 May 1889 - 14 May 1974) was a leading psychiatrist, theorist and educator. During his lifetime Dr. Moreno was recognized at Harvard University as one of the greatest social scientists in the world. Dr. Moreno grew up in Vienna at time of great intellectual creativity and political turmoil. The founder of Psychodrama, Sociometry and the foremost pioneer of Group Psychotherapy, Moreno studied medicine, mathematics, and philosophy at the University of Vienna, becoming an M.D. in 1917. He had rejected Freudian theory while still a medical student, and became interested in the potential of group settings for therapeutic practice

---

[9] Abraham Maslow (1st April 1908 - 8 June1970)[9] was an American psychologist who pioneered humanistic psychology **a**nd developed ideas related to a hierarchy of needs.

[10] **Stanislav Grof** (born July 1, 1931) is **a** psychiatrist, one of the founders of the field of transpersonal psychology and a pioneering researcher into the use of non-ordinary states of consciousness for purposes of exploring, healing, and obtaining growth and insights into the human psyche.

[11] Anthony Sutich (1907-1976) was a pioneer in Transpersonal Psychology. The Transpersonal Institute (parent corporation of the Journal of Transpersonal Psychology and the Association for Transpersonal Psychology) has been organized by Anthony Sutich to investigate unitive
consciousness, peak experiences, mystical awakenings, self-actualization and transcendence.

[12] Numineux : from Numen : sacred

[13] Gilbert Pierre and Anne-Christine Pierre « Paroles d'une autiste muette » éditions L'harmattan 2010

[14] Bernard Montaud, « César l'éclaireur », Dervy editions

[19] « Les Voix de la main, faire de ses blessures le levier de sa réalisation » Dervy editions.
[16] " Et si nos ancêtres parlaient à travers nous », Editions Quintessence 2008

---

[17] Marie Vialard-Hauser and Lucile Vialard, In the book « Tu nous as ouvert les yeux », from the edition « L'écrit du cœur » 2011.

[18] Jean Vanier, (born September 10, 1928) is a Canadian Catholic philosopher turned theologian, humanitarian, and the founder of L'Arche, an international federation of group homes for people with

developmental disabilities and those who assist them;

A PATH TO SELF

Thanks

I would like to thank all of the people who trusted me and entrusted me with their hand during one or more sessions.

Thanks to Lucile, Muriel, Anne-Christine, Léa, Mayann, Annick, Benoit, Timothée, for the wisdom transmitted through their texts.

Also thank you to Juliette, Alain and Margaux for their love and wisdom. I had the joy of accompanying them and now they have returned to Unity above this space and time.

I also send my gratitude to Seymour Brussel, Dr. Rodolphe Meyer, Aude Zeller, Anne-Catherine Dufour, Emmanuel Ransford and Marie Vialard-Hauser for their participation in the AIC seminars. Their presence and help is precious and what I have learned with them has participated in the creation of this book.

Thanks to Pierre Weil for all I learned from him and also Michael Roads who allows me to question myself again and again while constantly enlarging my references.

Also, an immense thank you to Ann King for her very appropriate translation.

A PATH TO SELF

<u>Website:</u>

In French:

www.communication-profonde.com

In English:

www.innercommunication.fr